I0453163

2024 Pastoral Statistics

75% of pastors: report feeling "extremely stressed" or "highly stressed" in their roles.

Around 80% of pastors: believe their ministry negatively affects their families.

Between 60-80% of pastors: who enter ministry will not remain in it after 10 years.

70% of pastors: report working between 55-75 hours per week.

A large percentage of pastors: lack a close confidant or mentor within their ministry.

THE LAND OF COPE

A Pastoral Leadership Guide to Accountability

Rev. Leonard Huggins, Jr.

Cope, South Carolina

The Land of Cope: A Leadership Guide to Accountability
Copyright©2025 by Rev. Leonard Huggins

For more information, contact Rev. Leonard Huggins, Jr. at authorleonardhuggins@gmail.com.

Cover by: Sharon Lewis-Ruff, The Planner Consulting
Editing by: Sharon Lewis-Ruff
Formatting by: Wisdom by 30 Literary Group

ISBN: 979-8-9942619-0-3
ISBN Digital: 979-8-9942619-0-3

Author's Previous Work

Coming Out the Huddle uses the comparison of the church's mission to the game of football. Author, Rev. Leonard Huggins Jr., encourages, inspires and shares a game plan with four strategic moves that will build you in becoming a committed Christian, prepared for the game of life. This book is a reminder that the huddle is only a meeting place to strategize play execution. Like the huddle, the church is also a meeting place used to fuel in carrying out the Great Commission.

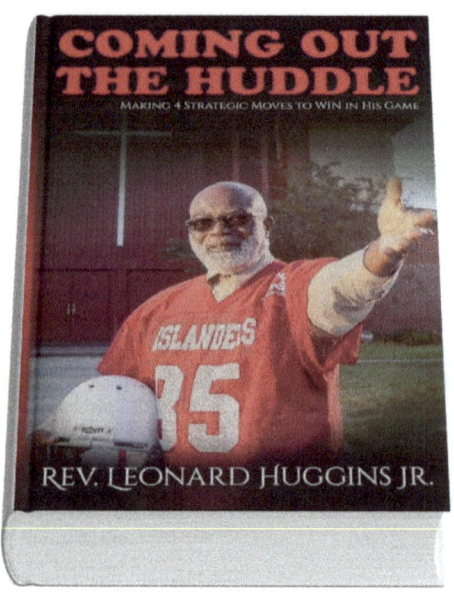

This book is a testimony, a blueprint, and a call to action.

When God called me to pastor, He didn't send me to churches that were full, He sent me to places that were broken, struggling, and in need of revival. I have walked into quiet sanctuaries where hope had nearly dried up. I've seen empty pews, discouraged members, and divided leadership. But I have also seen what happens when people take God at His word.

This book is not about theory. It is about experience. Every chapter is rooted in real-life ministry, the kind that happens outside the spotlight, deep in the trenches. I write not as someone who has all the answers, but as someone who has been through the fire, sat in the meetings, and prayed in the midnight hour for God to breathe life back into His church.

If you're a pastor, a church leader, or even a faithful member wondering why your church is stuck, this book is for you. If you're dealing with low attendance, spiritual complacency, financial strain, or resistant leadership, you're not alone. God has a revival plan, but it requires order, obedience, and boldness.

We'll talk about stewardship, prayer, leadership conflict, spiritual warfare, and how to teach people the Word so they live it and *not* just hear it. We'll deal with the reality of church hurt and the resistance that often comes when you're trying to lead God's people forward.

More than anything, this is a book about *faith*, the kind that moves mountains, revives ministries, and brings dead things back to life.

Let's rebuild the church, one act of obedience at a time.

66

Malachi 3:7

7 Even from the days of your fathers ye are gone away from mine ordinances, and have not kept them. Return unto me, and I will return unto you, saith the Lord of hosts. But ye said, Wherein shall we return?

Editorial Reviews

Blending the richness of Southern tradition, church culture, and generational wisdom, this book is a powerful reminder of what it means to lead with integrity and faith. The author's sermon to graduating students is a standout gem; honest, humorous, deeply spiritual, and unforgettable. Every page speaks with a voice of experience and love, challenging the reader to rise higher and walk worthy of their calling.

Deeply rooted in biblical truth and everyday wisdom, this is a must-read for graduates, ministry leaders, and anyone shaping the future with faith as their foundation.

chapter one

66

Luke 2:25

And, behold, there was a man in Jerusalem, whose name was Simeon; and the same man was just and devout, waiting for the consolation of Israel: and the Holy Ghost was upon him.

Chapter One - GROWING UP IN COPE, SC

Proverbs 3:1–2, 5–8 (KJV)
My son, forget not my law; but let thine heart keep my commandments: For length of days, and long life, and peace, shall they add to thee... Trust in the LORD with all thine heart; and lean not unto thine own understanding. In all thy ways acknowledge him, and he shall direct thy paths. Be not wise in thine own eyes: fear the LORD, and depart from evil... and marrow to thy bones.

As I reflect on my life, I can't help but go back to my roots—growing up in Cope, South Carolina, on my grandfather's rented 300-acre farm. Life was *hard* work. Every single day, from sunup to sundown, we had something to do. I went barefoot many days, chopping and picking cotton, planting gardens, making syrup, butchering hogs, cutting wood for cooking and heating, milking cows, and feeding the animals.

But we found joy, too—hunting rabbits, picking plums and blackberries, swimming in the creek, shooting marbles, playing football, softball, and basketball. The only rest came during thunderstorms. When the lightning struck, the old folks would say, *"The Lord is talking—be still, be quiet, or go lay down."*

We didn't sleep in beds unless it was nighttime or we were sick. Beds were sacred—made up neatly and left untouched during the day. When you woke up, you made that bed with care. No questions asked.

Monday through Saturday, we worked. Up by 6 a.m., wash up, feed the chickens, cows, hogs, mule, and horse, then eat breakfast and hit the fields. I was just six years old, riding on the back of that tractor with my daddy, pulling grass off the plow at the end of the row.

Sunday? That was the Lord's Day. No exceptions. We went to Sunday School and Worship Service like clockwork. On the 1st and 3rd Sundays, we attended Canaan Episcopal Methodist Church—now Canaan United Methodist Church. My grandfather was the church treasurer for many years. The 2nd and 4th Sundays, we were at Good Hope African Methodist Episcopal Church with my daddy, who served as a Class Leader.

It was in those sanctuaries I learned to pray the Lord's Prayer, say grace before eating, recite scripture, and memorize the 23rd Psalm—"*The Lord is my shepherd...*"—before I even knew what a shepherd really was.

Every Sunday evening at 6 p.m., the Usher Board Service would gather several churches together. Children and youth recited speeches from memory (you better not have a piece of paper), sang solos, or played instruments. And our mamas would whisper, "***You better not make me ashamed.***" Each church marched around the aisles, shouting, singing, and laying money on the table. After the secretary read out how much each church gave, the offering stayed right there at the host church.

The third week in July was the highlight of the year—*Summer Revival*, or what we called "Big Meeting Time." Monday through Friday nights were revival services, and every Friday night was the night to go to the mourner's bench and confess Jesus as **Lord**. If you confessed, the guest preacher would talk with you that Friday evening. On Sunday, after Worship Service, dinner was served outside on long tables and from car trunks.

The men made cold lemonade in 50-gallon wooden barrels, and the evening service started back up around 3 or 4 p.m.

And folks came back home from up North and all over. They brought with them their Big Meeting offering. Because they were taught, *"Don't forget your home church when God blesses you. You better give God some of that money before He makes you spend it elsewhere."*

When my daddy passed away, I was only ten. On the 2nd and 4th Sundays, my brother and I had to attend the Holiness Church with our Aunt Lillie. Sometimes we didn't get home until 4 or 5 p.m., missing the sandlot football or baseball games where the girls would cheer us on.

School was no different from church. Our parents believed that education and hard work were your ticket to freedom and success. "Ain't nobody gonna give you nothing. You've got to work for it. Learn something, get your own." They believed every child could learn if they paid attention—because God *didn't* make no dumb children. Teachers were like parents, and if you got out of line, your behind was going to get it—at school and again when you got home.

The teachers had full permission to discipline. If they called home, your parents didn't ask for your side—they trusted that teacher. "If I have to come to that schoolhouse…" was all the warning you needed.

By high school, if a child wasn't going to college, the guidance counselor sent them to Denmark Area Trade School. You either had a job offer waiting at graduation, or you were prepared to start your own business.

And for some, the recommendation was the military—so they could learn discipline and responsibility.

Luke 2:52 says, "And Jesus increased in wisdom and stature, and in favor with God and man."

And that's me—growing in wisdom, not just spiritually, but practically.
 In church and school.
 In work and worship.
 In plowing fields and preaching pulpits.
 That's how my leadership was formed.

True leadership is forged in the quiet lessons of discipline, humility, and service. From sunup to sundown, we learn that integrity begins at home—in how we work, how we honor God, and how we respect those who guide us. The foundation laid by elders, built on faith, family, and responsibility, teaches us that leadership is not about titles, but about character. A leader listens when the Lord is speaking, rises early to serve, respects authority, and carries forward wisdom with grace and conviction.

We lead best when we remember where we came from—and who kept us.

As leaders, we must remember:
- We are called to work hard, stay humble, and honor those who came before us.
- We are responsible for growing in wisdom, not just in stature.
- We must model consistency in worship, discipline in duty, and courage in accountability.

The seeds of leadership were sown in the rows we once plowed, and they're watered by faith, integrity, and truth. Never forget—God didn't make any dumb children, and He surely didn't call any lazy leaders. He's looking for willing hearts, not just loud voices.

chapter two

66

I am counting on You
to do the GODLY thing,
the RIGHT thing. To be
somebody... don't be
the problem, be the
problem SOLVER.

Chapter Two - THE CALL AND SEMINARY

"And the child Samuel ministered unto the Lord before Eli. And the word of the Lord was precious in those days; there was no open vision." —1 Samuel 3:1 (KJV)

I always considered myself a pretty decent person—didn't get into much trouble, treated folks right, especially the elders. They used to say, "That boy gon' be somebody one day," just because of the way I carried myself and how I helped out.

At seventeen, I was already serving on the church trustee committee. I'll never forget when the District Superintendent at the Edisto Fork Charge Conference congratulated me for being the youngest trustee in the entire South Carolina Conference. By the time I was twenty and attending Claflin University, I was the Sunday School Superintendent for a year.

Now, the church folks had their eyes on my brother, Horace. They said he walked, talked, sang, and looked like a preacher. But Horace would always laugh and point at me, "They talkin' about you, not me. You just scared." And maybe I was. But I've always been honest, straightforward, and meant what I said.

My pastor at the time, the late Rev. Warren Jenkins of Canaan UMC, saw something in me. He said, *"Son, I see a minister in you."* I told him, *"No sir, you mean my brother."* But Rev. Jenkins wouldn't let it go. After I graduated from Claflin and worked the night shift as an orderly at the hospital, my nursing supervisor tried to steer me toward nursing school. I said, *"No ma'am, that's not for me."*

I worked a year at Utica Tools, where they promised me an

office job. But one day, they said, "*Your mouth is too loud.*" I got married to Dearie the day after Thanksgiving. My cousin and I tried to enlist in the Army that June, but there wasn't a slot open until October.

And here's where God really stepped in.

Rev. Jenkins heard I was heading to the Army and asked me to come by his house. "*I still believe there's a call on your life. Why not go to seminary? Get your Master of Divinity in Parish Ministry. Go to Gammon Theological Seminary in Atlanta. There's more than just preaching—you can do a lot with that degree.*"

I told him again, "*You mean my brother. He's not ready.*" But he pressed: "*Just give it a year, and I believe God will show you. Your wife can get her Master's at the AU Center while y'all live in the married student housing. Dr. Major Jones, the Dean of Gammon, is my friend. He'll look out for you.*"

The first year at Gammon was **no joke**. Students from all over the world, smarter than I was, came ready. The professors would say, "If you can make it here, you can pastor and teach anywhere in the world."

I got angry... angry at how behind I felt. I called home and told Mama I was coming back. She said, "*You bet not. Don't you make me ashamed. You better hit your knees, read that Bible, and ask God for help. You got a wife and a baby on the way, and the DS is giving you a church in June. Don't you come back here without that degree—do you hear me?*"

"*Yes, ma'am.*"
"*Good. Now I'm coming down there to check on you.*"

"No ma'am, I'll be alright."

I had to take a remedial English writing course in my first semester. I'll never forget having to write the word "experience" 100 times because I misspelled it. But I joined a study group— seven of us, each assigned a section to break down and teach the others. My grades improved, and I got off probation.

One African brother in the group once told us, *"You Americans don't realize the opportunity you have. You're too lazy. You take it all for granted."* That shook me. I realized I had to do better with what God had given me.

Dr. Isaac Clark, our Homiletics professor, made us preach in front of our peers. We were graded on what we said, how we said it, and why we said it. That class was terrifying and humbling. I got a C and was grateful to pass.

Dr. Major Jones, the president, said, *"Preachers, you must know the book—but more importantly, know how to speak to people who've been there before you. They don't care what degrees you have—they want to know if you care."*
That stuck with me.

I worked during seminary cleaning dorms, cutting grass, earning just enough to buy a little blue Volkswagen Beetle. Every Friday, I'd drive to Pendleton, SC, to pastor my three churches and then head back to Atlanta Sunday night or early Monday morning. The South Carolina Conference had some of the best preachers; they could *hoop* and tell the story. At our weekly "powwow" service on Wednesdays, when it was my turn to preach, folks said, *"We didn't know you had it in you. You so quiet. You gon' be a good preacher."*

"And the child Samuel ministered unto the LORD before Eli..."
– 1 Samuel 3:1 (KJV)

Every calling has a beginning—often quiet, sometimes unnoticed, and almost always wrapped in a sense of "not me, Lord." Like Samuel, many of us are raised in the presence of God long before we recognize His voice. We serve, we help, we grow—but the calling? That still feels too big.
Yet God sees beyond what we think we are and calls out what He knows we can become.

Your journey reminds us that God's purpose is not limited by our past, our doubts, or even our detours. Mentors like Rev. Jenkins, mothers who refuse to let us quit, and professors who stretch our thinking are all divine instruments sharpening us for the call. The seminary, the sermons, the setbacks, and the sleepless nights—all were shaping seasons, not stopping signs.

When you look back, you see how far God brought you—not just into ministry, but into a deeper understanding of yourself. That's the power of grace: it doesn't just call us, it keeps us.

Let this be an encouragement: You may not feel ready. You may question if you're enough. But if God is calling, He's already equipped you. And He'll place people along your path who see what you can't yet see in yourself.

chapter three

"

Increase.
Stabilize.
Lift.

This chapter reflects the *honest* journey of my start as a pastor, one filled with both progress and pruning.

There will be moments when you begin to see the fruit of your labor, when your love for the people runs deep, and yet, you're called to pack up and move again. It's not easy. The shifting can feel like a loss, especially when you're just beginning to make headway. But every assignment carries a purpose. Even in the discomfort, God is working something greater through you.

The challenge is not just in the relocation, it's in discerning the reason. *Ask God*, "Why here? Why now?" and trust that your obedience is never wasted. Each place, each group of people, and each season is shaping the pastor, and the purpose, within you.

Chapter Three - THE APPOINTMENTS

My first appointment, called a student appointment, was at North Charge, where I was assigned to serve two churches. I received an elder's salary and followed an elder who had served there for twelve years, yet never truly lived among the people.

At the time, I was attending Gammon Seminary. My wife and I were expecting our first child, and I was their first young pastor. Six months in, during the charge conference, the church voted to continue paying me an elder's salary. However, the District Superintendent (DS) objected.

"Leonard is a student pastor," he said. "He can't be making more than other student pastors."
But then, the Chairman of the Administrative Board raised his hand and said, "We love our pastor. Our members are returning, giving more, and he can preach."

The DS didn't like it, but he couldn't override them. Still, by June, I was moved. A three-person leadership team had been running the church, and I upset one of them. They ran to the DS, who used another church's prior request for a pastor change as justification to move me again.

APPOINTMENT TWO: Roseville Parish

My second charge was in the country: three churches, known as the Roseville Parish. I was still in seminary.

The DS told me, "Just preach on Sundays and bury the dead-on Saturdays or Sundays. Your education is your priority." **But** trouble soon found me. The larger church wanted me to preach all four Sundays without a pay increase, and I refused to support their plan to merge with the two smaller churches and build on their property. Tensions rose.

One Sunday morning, the choir refused to sing the hymn of praise listed in the bulletin, though they had seen it in advance. One of the church bosses marched to the pulpit, but I stood calmly, three steps above him.

"Turn him loose," I told the member restraining him. "He's not a boy." They let him go, and he stormed out the side door. I was ready to hit him with the Holy Bible if I had to. After the choir finished their own selection, while the congregation chuckled, I turned to the pianist and said, "*Play What a Friend We Have in Jesus*. Let's have church."

Soon after, the church requested an elder, and I was moved again.

APPOINTMENT THREE: Pendleton Charge (Anderson District)

I was now closer to Atlanta and still finishing seminary. The DS said again, "Your education is the priority."

There was no parsonage for my family, so the church rented a house in town, right across from one of the churches. They wanted me to bring the youth back. But then came an unexpected test: the airport wanted Bethel Grove's land to expand.

Every Sunday, the noise of planes interrupted worship. We negotiated to protect the gravesite and sold the land. We then merged Bethel Grove and Mt. Zion, forming Central UMC, and built a new church with classrooms, bathrooms, a kitchen, and a fellowship hall. I was still in seminary. My wife worked at a daycare, and our son attended it. Spiritually, physically, and financially, it was a challenge. But in four years, with help from the South Carolina Conference, we raised the money and completed the church.

The DS said, "Leonard, you're amazing... a builder, a student, a preacher." I replied, "I know the Lord. I'm a praying preacher. And with God, all things are possible." I had good members— and difficult ones—that kept me on my knees, seeking God's direction in placing the right people in leadership. I also leaned on my spiritual father and fellow pastors.

Bishop Roy Clark preached the Consecration Service for our new church.

APPOINTMENT FOUR: Bennettsville

In Bennettsville Parish, I was responsible for three churches: Shiloh, St. Micheal, Smyrna. During that time, I became the Director of Bennettsville – Cheraw Cooperative Parish Ministry consisting of nine other churches.

Shiloh and Smyrna were rural churches, and St. Micheal was the town church.

Shiloh was renovated with a vestibule, two restrooms, a fellowship hall, kitchen, and a pastor's study.

St. Micheal became a *station church*. More Smyrna young adults put in leadership positions in the church under my leadership; it set a record.

I was the first African-America promoted to chairman of Marlboro County Democratic Party.

A Call to Greater Responsibility

Word spread... members from a larger, historical church downtown attended three of our services and were impressed.

They asked the DS if I could become their pastor. "We need someone who can bring the youth back," they said. The DS called me in, offering a new appointment at Thompson Centennial and New Harmony, with a $6,000 increase in salary and a parsonage next to the church. The members were professionals: principals, teachers, a doctor, a social services leader, and funeral directors.

At the PPRC meeting, they shared their hopes. Then the DS asked if I had anything to say. "Yes," I said. "I'm a country preacher. I may not cross all the T's or dot all the I's. I may break the English language." They laughed. "You're the preacher we want."

I outlined my worship plan: 1st Sundays: High church—Holy Communion and the Senior Choir Other Sundays: Gospel, spirituals, and hymns. Each week featured a different choir: Men's, Children & Youth, Young Adults, and Combined Choirs on 5th Sundays. We added a Tithing Cross Box at the front of the church, where members brought their offerings to the Lord.

I told them, "When you come to this church, expect something to happen. Let's have church. It's Showtime!"

APPOINTMENT FIVE: Bamberg Parish

Two churches.
One in town, one in the country.
We were in a building committee meeting when the chairman got angry because I sided with the group to renovate the old church sign instead of buying a new one like he wanted.

He stood up and said, "I'm going to get my Uzi and blow you away." I calmly said, "I got mine under the front seat. I'll drop you before you get to your truck."

The vice-chair quickly interrupted, "Rev, he's not worth killing." Everyone burst out laughing. We prayed and went with the committee's decision. Later, Dr. Joan and Mrs. Etta Kennedy donated $500. The SC Conference gave $50,000. Bishop Joseph Bethea preached the consecration.

But once again, some older members didn't like that we replaced the long-time musician who couldn't play contemporary music. Complaints went to the DS, and I was moved, *this time*, to a church that wanted to build.

My appointment journey continued at Friendship Church, a church that wasn't doing so well financially. It meant a $5000 salary cut for me. The District Superintendent (DS) told me to ride in his car to the church and not to mention anything about the salary reduction. He said, "They need a new church and have a membership of over 600 plus, *just* work with them."

When we arrived, there were more than nine Pastor Parish Relations Committee members present. I said, "Sir, there are more than the usual committee members here," and he replied, "That's alright, let them stay." After they finished talking about what they wanted me to help them do, especially building a new church, they admitted they didn't have any money. They wanted help getting the young people back in church and contributing financially. They said, "We heard about your work at the other church and at a new church start."

When it was my time to talk, I said, "Yes, I know where the money is." The treasurer lady asked, "Where?" I pointed and said, "In those pocketbooks on the floor and those wallets on your left hip." Everybody burst into laughter.

"I am a tithing and offering preacher, and I will teach and preach on how God will provide. I need all leaders to pay their 10 percent first, then teach the members to do the same. If not, the Nomination Committee is going to have some serious words with you in October. That's the preacher you need."

Then I told them about the $5,000 salary cut. The chairman of the trustee board immediately said, "We will pay that $5,000, Mr. DS." The DS got angry with me for mentioning it, because he told me not to bring it up.

We built the new church in four years and bought a new parsonage within my first two months there. We raised $500,000 in two years to build the new church. When the conference offered the church $50,000, I told the treasurer lady to send it back. She said, "No, Rev, you're going crazy!"

After ten years, the DS moved me from Friendship because some members had petitioned to have me moved. They told the Bishop there was no money in the treasury. But when I met with the Bishop and three DSs, I showed them the bank statements: $40,000 in the regular checking account and $60,000 in the building fund account. I had copies of everything I had accomplished at the church.

The Bishop, after seeing the evidence, asked me to stay one more year, but I said "No. The first thing the new leaders are going to do is cut the salary. Move me, I'll take the salary cut because there will be no peace or growth in the church if I go back."

APPOINTMENT SIX: New Covenant UMC

I was sent to Bowman, SC, to a station church called New Covenant UMC, where the highway separated the parsonage from the church. It meant a $4,000 salary cut. I preached and taught about tithes and offerings to the leaders first, then to the congregation. One of the elderly leaders said, "You are the preacher we need now!! I'll follow as long as you preach and *teach* tithes and offering."

In five years, we raised $200,000 to build a fellowship hall and add a new addition to the front of the church with two lounges, two bathrooms, and a large vestibule.

APPOINTMENT SEVEN: John Island Parish

I was sent to John Island Parish, two churches on Main Road seven miles apart, and New Webster UMC on Walhalla Island. The Bishop asked me to merge St. James and Bethlehem, build them a new church on Bethlehem's property (since they had 19½ acres of land), increase the salary, get them a parsonage, and be a voice in the community because taxes on people's land were being raised.

Bethlehem and St. James merged, becoming Bethlehem-St. James UMC. The parish bought a $300,000 parsonage in the third year, and Bethlehem-St. James church raised $221,000 for their new building. The salary was increased every year, but I was removed from the Parish before I could complete the new church for Bethlehem-St. James.

I was moved because the DS said I had accomplished more in four years than expected.
When I asked why, he said, "*Even Moses didn't make it to the Promised Land with the Israelites.*"

I responded, "Now tell me why you're moving me! I haven't finished what the Bishop told me to do, and that was to merge them and prepare for the new church."

"I'm glad you asked that question, God told Moses why he wasn't going into the Promised Land."

"Now tell me why you're moving me! I haven't finished what the Bishop told me to do, and that was to merge them and prepare for the new church."

APPOINTMENT EIGHT: St. George Parish

I moved to the St. George Parish, which consisted of two rural churches, Shady Grove and St. Mark. and Trinity Church in the town of St. George, SC.

In my third year, Shady Grove Church became a station church. The majority wanted it, though a minority was against it. There are always going to be crowds wanting to keep things the same—no growth.

I retired from Shady Grove UMC after 45 years in Parish Ministry. I learned that if the pastor shines, then the church will shine too.

"You did not choose Me, but I chose you and appointed you so that you might go and bear fruit—fruit that will last..."
— John 15:16 (NIV)

There have been seasons in my life where I was moved without explanation, misunderstood without cause, and placed in assignments that didn't make sense at first glance. But over time, I've learned a holy truth: God never wastes an appointment.

Whether I was sent to a storefront, a sanctuary, or a struggling church, God had already gone before me. I wasn't just filling a pulpit—I was fulfilling a purpose.

The appointments were rarely about my comfort. They were about God's call. Not every place welcomed me with open arms. Not every journey was easy. But in each one, God stretched me, shaped me, and showed me that the assignment was never just about me. It was about the people, the legacy, the healing, and the harvest He intended to bring through my obedience.

When you know you're appointed for a reason bigger than yourself, you stop seeking validation from people and start walking in God's affirmation. You become less concerned with popularity and more anchored in purpose. You understand that where you are is not by accident—it's by divine design.

If you're in a place that feels difficult or unfamiliar, don't lose heart. You are appointed.

Not for applause.
Not for comfort.
But for impact.
For fruit that will last.

So lead, serve, love, and obey.

Because your appointment is tied to someone else's breakthrough. And that, beloved, is bigger than you.

chapter four

Chapter Four - PARSONAGES

"I have planted, Apollos watered; but God gave the increase."
-1 Corinthians 3:6 (KJV)

Over the course of my ministry, I've been assigned to several appointments, each with its own challenges, blessings, and lessons. At every stop, I made it a point not just to serve the congregation, but to leave things better than I found them. I purchased three parsonages, renovated two with brand-new furniture, and rented two more, making sure each one became a home, not just a house.

Because here's the truth: as pastors, we're not just planting seeds in the pulpit—we're also called to plant peace in our homes.

I've learned that your greatest ministry doesn't start at the altar. It starts at your address.

If you have a family, you must prioritize their joy, their stability, and their belonging. Ministry is heavy enough. Your home should be a refuge, not another battlefield. Your spouse shouldn't have to compete with the church for your time, and your children shouldn't grow up resenting the calling on your life because it pulled you away from theirs.

You can't expect to lead others well if you're leading your household poorly. Scripture tells us plainly that the increase comes from God. But it's up to us to be faithful stewards—to plant, to water, to tend to the things and people He's entrusted to us.

So yes, I made those houses into homes. Not just for me and mine, but for the next family that would come through. Because legacy leadership doesn't think just about today, it thinks about tomorrow.

Let your family feel the fruit of your calling, not the weight of it.

- Love them out loud.
- Serve them first.
- Honor them publicly.
- Protect their peace privately.

And always remember: *your first ministry walks through your front door every evening.*

Parsonage: Your Children

"Train up a child in the way he should go: and when he is old, he will not depart from it." Proverbs 22:6 (KJV)

One of the quiet burdens many pastors carry, but rarely talk about, is the fear that our children won't follow in our footsteps. We pray, we hope, we lead by example, and still... they may choose a different road. And you know what? That's okay.

Our job isn't to manufacture their calling.
Our job is to affirm their identity, in Christ and in themselves, even if it doesn't look like ours.

I've seen too many ministers unintentionally wound their children by measuring them against their own anointing. They confuse legacy with duplication. But God is too creative for copies. He made your child with their own gifts, voice, and purpose. Your pulpit may be the platform, but their purpose may bloom in a classroom, courtroom, film set, or tech lab. Ministry isn't limited to a microphone, it can show up in how they treat people, how they create, and how they lead.

Let your child know that their value isn't rooted in their proximity to the pulpit, but in their connection to God.

- Speak life over them.
- Celebrate their passions.
- Be present at their games, shows, and presentations, even when Sunday morning wore you out.
- Listen to what they don't say.
- And for heaven's sake, never make them feel like they're competing with the church for your love.

Just because they don't walk your path doesn't mean they're lost. Sometimes, the most powerful way to minister to your children is simply by being their parent, *not their pastor*.

When your child feels seen, heard, and loved as they are, they won't have to *search* for affirmation in all the wrong places. Your presence, your words, and your consistent belief in them becomes a seed that God will water in His timing.

Ministry starts at home.
And it grows best in a house where love isn't earned; it's just given.

Parsonage: Your Spouse

"Two are better than one; because they have a good reward for their labour." Ecclesiastes 4:9 (KJV)

Behind every pastor's robe, collar, or title is someone who knows them beyond the applause and altar calls. That someone, more often than not, is a spouse who has prayed with you in the midnight hour, helped pick up the pieces after church hurt, and stood beside you while you poured yourself out like oil Sunday after Sunday.

Let me say this plainly:
Your spouse is not your assistant. They are your partner in purpose.

Now, I know tradition can make that tricky. Some folks still expect the First Lady to sit in the front row, wear a hat, and smile through it all. But leadership has evolved, and God is showing us that ministry works best when it flows from a place of mutual respect, transparency, and shared vision.

You can preach deliverance, but if your spouse is drowning in silence or feels unseen, you've missed the mark. One of the greatest gifts you can give your ministry is a healthy, affirmed marriage.

Make time to laugh together, outside of church business.
Check in with their heart, not just their schedule.
Honor their voice in decision-making, especially when it affects the whole household.
Encourage their calling, even if it doesn't mirror yours.
Pray together not just before services, but in the quiet, ordinary days too.

Your spouse was appointed to walk beside you, not behind you.

When God called you, He also knew the support you would need. And in that covenant bond, He gave you more than a companion, He gave you someone with the spiritual and emotional capacity to hold your weary moments, lift your head, and remind you of who you are when you forget.

The church *may* know your gift.

But your spouse? They know your grace.
Honor that. Protect that. Build with that.
Because the ministry that thrives most... is the one that starts at home.

Parsonage: When Leadership Hurts at Home

Leadership is a calling, but it's also *a weight*. And sometimes, even the strongest shoulders grow tired. Whether you're a pastor, a parent, a principal, or simply the one everyone else depends on, there comes a moment when mistakes are made, tempers fray, and even the most faithful leaders lose their way. But I need to remind you of something important: missteps don't disqualify you from God's plan; they just mean *you're human*.

Leadership burnout can quietly creep in. It shows up in short words at home, skipped prayers, and the silent guilt of knowing your family sometimes gets your leftovers instead of your best. But hear me: You can recover.

Here are a few truths to hold onto when leadership breaks down at home:

1. ***Acknowledge it honestly.***
Don't try to hide it. Your family already knows something's off. Sit down and say, "I've been stretched thin, and I haven't been the leader I should be at home. I'm sorry." There's strength in humility.

2. ***Reconnect with your first ministry—your family.***
Before the pulpit, the platform, or the paycheck, God gave you your family. Don't neglect them trying to save the world. Saving your home is saving the world—one life at a time.

3. ***Get still.***
Burnout often means you've been moving too fast for too long. Take time to rest in God. Not to produce. Not to perform. Just to be His child. The world will still spin while you sit in silence.

4. Rebuild with small bricks.

Trust isn't rebuilt overnight. It comes through consistency. Praying again together. Laughing again. Listening without rushing. Giving your presence, not just your provision.

5. Get help if you need it.

Jesus had disciples. Moses had Aaron. You're not supposed to lead alone. Don't suffer in silence. Whether it's counseling, mentorship, or simply a friend to talk to, reach out.

6. Let God restore your soul.

Psalm 23 doesn't say "He gives you more to do." It says, "He restores my soul." Leadership recovery isn't about doing more; it's about letting God do more in you.

To every leader who's ever felt guilty, tired, or ashamed: God hasn't forgotten you. Your calling still stands. Your family still matters. And you are still needed—not perfect, but present.

Your spouse is not your assistant—they are your partner in purpose.

They are not just helping you carry out your calling; they are part of that calling. You are a team, called to walk together, pray together, build together, and grow together. When you treat your spouse as an equal partner, not a background supporter, you honor not only them, but the God who joined you together.

Pause and ask yourself:
- Am I listening to their voice with the same weight I give to church leaders or ministry teams?
- Have I made room for their gifts, dreams, and spiritual insight to flourish?
- Are we still aligned, or have we slipped into roles instead of a relationship?

Ministry starts at home. Before the pulpit, before the meetings, before the titles—there's covenant. Protect it. Nurture it. Honor it.

Together, you're not just building a ministry. You're building a legacy.

chapter five

Chapter Five - HOW DID I LEAD?

I see myself as a democratic leader most of the time. I share information with the Lay Leader and the administrative board. I've always believed in having one-on-one meetings with each committee chairperson before they step into leading, after they've had time to consult with the pastor. There have also been times I've had to go straight to the congregation or a committee and say, "Here's where we are, and here's what needs to happen." But most of the time, I honor what the committee has voted on and try to lead with their consensus.

In my 45 years of pastoring, I've shepherded several churches that didn't want to move, didn't want to grow. They were satisfied doing the same thing over and over again. Year after year, I witnessed families fighting each other—not in their homes, but in the church. The sanctuary became a battleground for who was going to "run things." And when the pastor tried to break up the control that 2 or 3 families had over the leadership, trying to spread out responsibility fairly, that same pastor suddenly became the problem. Because in those churches, everyone was somebody's sister, cousin, uncle, or in-law.

Many refused to read the church guidelines, skipped out on Sunday school, Bible study, and training sessions, but were the loudest during Sunday service. Oh, they'd show up then. Sunday morning was showtime: who could "out-sing" or "out-shout" the other. That was the main event. But when it came time to sit down and reason together, to listen, to grow, to study, they had no interest.

Although they didn't know how to talk to each other anymore, yet, strangely enough, the giving would still increase.

Even when I worked with the Nominating Committee to bring in younger adult leaders, it didn't take long before they started following the footsteps of the older adults—some of the same habits, same backroom behavior, same passive resistance. It's hard to lead a church like that. Sometimes all you can do is preach, teach, and wait on God to move some of those headstrong, controlling folks out of the way.

The sacredness—the holiness—of the church isn't what it used to be. There are people in leadership who haven't accepted Jesus Christ as their personal Savior, yet they want to be in charge. They won't go to any training, won't grow in the Word, but they want a title. Churches today have gotten so worldly that anything goes, as long as you don't mess with me and my friends. That's the attitude.

They cover for each other. They won't say a word in the meeting, but as soon as it's over, the real conversation starts—in the parking lot or over the phone. They'll talk about it everywhere except where it counts.

But the truth is, the pastor is called, *mandated*, to hold the people accountable. Not to tradition, not to feelings, but to the truth.

And when that happens? Some of them pick up the phone and call the DS. And more often than not... the DS sides with them.

If you're a leader reading this, let me tell you: don't let mess linger. Don't let unresolved issues fester until they infect the whole body. If there's confusion, confront it in love. If there's division, deal with it in truth. If there's disorder in leadership, don't ignore it just to keep the peace—because fake peace is not God's peace.

Handle what needs to be handled—quickly, prayerfully, and with clarity. You are not just keeping order; you are protecting the witness of the church. Silence in the face of dysfunction is agreement. And leadership that avoids accountability is leadership that quietly surrenders its authority.

You've been called to lead, not to entertain, not to pacify. So stand up. Speak up. Clean it up. Let God back you up.

Punishment Appointments

"But as for you, ye thought evil against me, but God meant it unto good, to bring to pass, as it is this day, to save much people alive." -Genesis 50:20 (KJV).

Ministry will take you places. Some places you asked for… and some you didn't.

There were times in my journey when I felt I wasn't being appointed... *I was being punished*. I stood up for the church when some in leadership wanted to push through what the people never asked for. I spoke up when I was told what Black churches couldn't do. But I've learned this truth: *with a praying pastor and a willing people, a Black church can do anything God ordains.* Don't let small minds tell you what God-sized faith can't build.

I remember one appointment where I had just led a congregation in building a new sanctuary. But the District Superintendent wanted me moved *quietly*. Told me not to mention salary. Said nothing about the fact that I'd be taking a $6,000 pay cut, with two children and a wife at home. Thank God my wife worked for the Department of Social Services or we wouldn't have made it.

But I went because the church needed leadership. They wanted to grow, reach young people, and build a future. I agreed to serve, but I didn't hide the facts. I told them what I was sacrificing to be there.

And you know what happened?

The Chairman of the Trustees stood up and said, "I seen the church he just built. I make the motion we add that $6,000 back to his salary to keep Mrs. Huggins happy!" It was seconded, voted on, and passed. The whole room broke into laughter, but I knew then I wasn't alone. There was *favor* in the house.

That *favor* didn't mean the road was smooth.

We arrived at the parsonage and found it too small to hold our things, let alone our lives. Roaches ran up and down the walls that first night. My wife cried. The children laughed to keep from crying. I called the SPRC chair, and she said, "There's nothing I can do tonight." We spent the next two months in a motel. School was out, and we had nowhere to settle.

I remember another time, same story, parsonage too small, closets couldn't hold my robes, and vermin made themselves more comfortable than we could. This time, the DS told me I had to stay there. We had a heated discussion. His wife happened to be with him that day, and she said,
"Honey, you know you wouldn't stay here. Why are you trying to make Leonard stay here?"

She told the truth.

I prayed. Then I talked to the church. We found a corner lot, a half-acre for $120,000. A Senator helped us. The church paid cash for it. The Chair of the District Building & Location Committee said, "*You don't need a committee. This house is made from the best materials. Buy it now.*"

We bought it.

That same church?

They raised half a million dollars to build their new sanctuary in just two years. But not every appointment ended like that.

At one church, I told the DS I was taking a $6,000 salary cut. He got mad and canceled the appointment altogether. That church still doesn't have a new building to this day.

And then there was the time a building committee meeting turned into a near stand-off. One of the members got upset because we voted to renovate the old church sign instead of buying a brand-new one.
He said, *"I'm going home to get my Uzi and come back here and blow you and that member away."*

I said, *"I've got mine under the front seat of my car. And before you make it to your truck, I'll drop you in your tracks."*

Everybody laughed, but I knew that spirit wasn't joking. One member said, "No Rev, he's not worth killing."
Still, I stood firm and said, *"Let's pray, and we're going with the committee's decision. Amen."*

Ministry can test your sanity, your marriage, and your call. You'll have to navigate church politics, leadership egos, and spiritual warfare—sometimes all in the same day. But if you stay faithful and plant what God tells you to plant, He'll bring the increase.

It won't always come easy. But it will come.
Stay grounded. Speak the truth. And lead, even when it feels like you're being sent to dry ground. Because sometimes, it's in those rocky places that God **sends** the rain.

Low Membership

"I can do all things through Christ which strengtheneth me."
Philippians 4:13 (KJV)

When I arrived at that church, the membership was low. The pews were mostly empty, the energy was low, and the people had grown weary. But I knew one thing for sure, God had not brought me there to maintain a dying church. He brought me there to help lead a revival, not just in numbers, but in spirit.

The first thing I did was study the church: its history, its leadership, what had worked in the past, and what hadn't. I asked the hard questions. Who truly wanted to see this church grow spiritually, numerically, and financially?

Then on Sunday morning, I didn't preach. I came down from the pulpit, sat among the people, and had a conversation. I asked them: What do you believe God wants to do here? My secretary took notes as a few brave members shared their hearts. That conversation became the message. Then I gave the altar call. I told them, *"Come back next Sunday. That's when I'll preach."*

When you're working with low membership, it's not just about filling the seats, it's about building faith. People need to understand that when they trust God and follow His Word, everything changes, including the size and strength of the congregation.

Malachi 3:10 – "Bring ye all the tithes into the storehouse... and prove me now herewith, saith the LORD of hosts..."

I taught and preached the principles of tithes and offerings.

I explained that when we are faithful stewards, God will bless us. I challenged the leaders and the members to give 10%, and to trust that God would multiply it, not just in their finances, but in their ministry.

But giving isn't just about money, it's about time, service, and inviting others to Christ. We launched membership training: Bible Study, Sunday School, and evangelism workshops. I taught them how to talk about their faith and how to invite people to church.

We anointed every pew with oil. We prayed for God to fill every seat. We laid hands on the members and asked God to break every stronghold that had kept the church stagnant. We asked God to cast out the spirit of division and defeat.

Good preaching draws people. Good music stirs their souls. But it's love, consistency, and vision that make them stay.

Once the members started seeing change, they became excited. They dared to go into the community and say, "*Come see what God is doing here.*" Some came. Some stayed. Some joined.

But let me be honest, many of the roadblocks didn't come from outside the church. They came from within, especially from the leadership. Some would agree with a plan in the meeting and then change their mind after the meeting. They'd say, "*Rev, we were here before you, and we'll be here after you.*"

That attitude blocked growth.
You can't build anything when leadership is double-minded. That confusion spreads to the congregation. And when the leaders stir up chaos, the members get discouraged.

That's why I made it clear: If you want to lead, show up for Sunday School, Bible Study, and leadership training not just in the church, but in the district too. If you don't, then sit down. *Don't block progress. Don't cause division.*

Sometimes I had to pull leaders aside and ask, "*What's really going on with you?*"

And yes, sometimes I had to talk plain, even a little ghetto, to get the message across: "*God needs you. The church needs you. But if you can't serve with the right heart, sit down. God always has a ram in the bush.*"

And just like that! God began to grow the church.

Special Favors

In ministry, one of the most difficult and delicate issues to navigate is the request for special favors. These requests often come from sincere hearts, but sometimes, they come from hearts seeking position, recognition, or personal benefit, not spiritual growth or church unity.

Let's be honest: special favors have caused more than a few pastors to stumble and more than a few churches to split. Why? Because when one person receives a benefit that does not edify the entire body, others begin to whisper, *"Rev. has favorites."* Before long, division creeps in, and what was once a house of unity becomes a house of murmuring, jealousy, and strife.

We must go back to Scripture and follow the example of Christ. In Matthew 20:20-28, the mother of James and John approached Jesus with a request:

"Promise me that one of my sons will sit at your right and the other at your left in your kingdom."
Jesus responded with wisdom and clarity:
"You don't know what you're asking. Are you able to drink from the cup I must drink from?"
They answered, "We are able."
Jesus replied, "You will indeed drink from my cup. But to sit at my right or left isn't mine to give. It is for those for whom it has been prepared by my Father."

What followed was a lesson for all the disciples and for us:
"Whoever wants to become great among you must be your servant... just as the Son of Man did not come to be served, but to serve." (vv. 26–28)

Jesus made it clear: requests for personal elevation are not the way of the kingdom. Leadership and favor come through service, not status.

When members approach asking for something that only benefits themselves—be it a title, a position, or influence—we must lovingly ask: **Will this benefit the whole church?**
If not, then it is not time. It may never be time.

Sometimes, those who make these requests have no idea the burden that comes with what they're asking. Jesus asked James and John, *"Can you drink from this cup?"* Many people *want* the crown without the cup. They desire the recognition but not the responsibility, the applause but not the anointing that comes through sacrifice.

When approached with these types of requests, we must pray. Not a personal prayer, but The Lord's Prayer—because it reminds us:

"Thy kingdom come, Thy will be done on earth as it is in heaven."
This is not about my will or your will, but God's will.

It is completely appropriate to say, *"Let's pray about that together. Let's ask the Holy Spirit to show us whether this is for the good of the church or just the good of a person."*

And let the Word speak for you. Scripture says in Romans 12:3 (NIV):
"Do not think of yourself more highly than you ought, but rather think of yourself with sober judgment, in accordance with the faith God has distributed to each of you."

Also in James 3:16 (KJV):
"For where envying and strife is, there is confusion and every evil work."

If we allow special favor to take root, it will bloom into division, jealousy, and broken fellowship. But when we walk in unity and humility, we honor God and keep the church focused on its mission.

So I say to every pastor and every member: the next time someone asks for something that benefits only themselves, respond with love and truth:
"*Will it bless the whole house? Let's pray and ask the Holy Spirit to lead us.*"

That way, we **remain** faithful stewards of God's people and protect the peace and unity of His Church.

Lord, give me the courage to confront what needs correcting.
Help me lead with both truth and grace.
Teach me to speak when silence feels easier.
And strengthen me to protect what is sacred—
not with fear, but with faith.

Amen.

chapter six

Chapter Six - LEADERSHIP & MINISTRY PLANNING

The strength of a church is not measured by the number of members filling the pews, but by the faithfulness, accountability, and follow-through of those who lead. A pastor *cannot*, and *should not*, run the church *alone*. That's why building a strong leadership team is essential for effective ministry and spiritual growth within the body of Christ.

Every chairperson of a committee and every committee member has a role to play, and those roles must come with clear assignments, a shared vision, and yearly goals. Too often, churches function on autopilot, going from Sunday to Sunday without a clear ministry plan. But God *is a God* of order, not chaos. Leadership without planning *leads* to confusion, miscommunication, and spiritual burnout.

Ministry planning should include:
- Clear objectives for each committee.
- A calendar of events and initiatives for the year.
- Defined responsibilities and timelines for execution.
- Regular communication with the pastor for spiritual covering and guidance.

It's not enough to simply accept a title. The church needs leaders, not placeholders. Accepting a position in the church is a commitment to serve faithfully, communicate clearly, and follow through with excellence. Leaders must work in unity with the pastor, not independently. Before carrying out any function, whether inside the church walls or in the community, seek the pastor's counsel and blessing.

If a pastor cannot attend a committee meeting, it is the leader's responsibility to **document and share meeting minutes**, so the pastor remains informed and spiritually connected to the work. No leader should ever make decisions that affect the body without the pastor's knowledge. That is not protocol—it is protection. It maintains alignment and ensures everything is done decently and in order.

This kind of leadership requires courage, responsibility, and spiritual maturity. That's why Paul reminded Timothy in 2 Timothy 1:7 (NLT):
"For God has not given us a spirit of fear and timidity, but of power, love, and self-discipline."

Leading a ministry or committee is not about control. It's about servant leadership, guided by love and the discipline to carry out the mission with integrity. If you are in leadership and unsure of how to move forward, ask yourself:
- Am I walking in fear or faith?
- Am I leading for status or to serve?
- Have I truly prayed and consulted with my pastor before taking action?

Church leadership should reflect Christ's character: loving, orderly, courageous, and humble. And it must operate in a system, a plan that empowers each ministry to grow and bear fruit.

A faithful leader is a gift to the church and a help to the pastor. So if you're called to lead, do it with excellence. If you're called to serve, do it with accountability. The body of Christ is strengthened when each part does its work, not independently, but in unity.

Let's stop giving out titles to those who aren't willing to carry the weight.

Sample Planning Outline

1. **January – Vision & Planning Month**
   - Meet with the Pastor to align on the ministry's spiritual vision and goals for the year.
   - Schedule all committee meetings for the year.
   - Set ministry objectives and develop a written plan of action.
   - Review past year's activities—what worked, what didn't.
   - Assign leadership roles and responsibilities within the committee.

2. **February – Team Building & Training**
   - Conduct a ministry retreat or training session for all committee members.
   - Clarify expectations, roles, and communication processes.
   - Pray for unity and discernment.
   - Develop a monthly devotional or spiritual encouragement rotation for team meetings.

3. **March – Outreach & Community Focus**
   - Plan a local outreach initiative or community engagement event.
   - Partner with other church ministries if needed.
   - Evaluate what resources and volunteers will be required.

4. **April – Quarterly Review**
   - Meet with the pastor to review Q1 goals and provide updates.
   - Adjust any timelines or expectations if needed.
   - Begin planning for summer events or special church-wide initiatives.

chapter seven

Chapter Seven - YOUR VOICE & THE COMMUNITY

"The voice of one crying in the wilderness, 'Prepare the way of the Lord, make His paths straight.'" -Matthew 3:3

As a minister of the Gospel, your assignment is not confined to the pulpit. You are called to be a voice... a consistent, trusted, godly presence in and for the community.

- **Be Present Where the People Are**

To build trust, the minister must live among the people. Residing in the community reflects commitment, builds relational credibility, and offers real-time opportunities to minister. When the community sees you at the grocery store, post office, school, and civic center, they feel seen, valued, and spiritually supported.

- **Show Up for Life's Milestones**

Attend funerals, even those outside your congregation. Your presence will minister louder than your words. Attend school events, sports games, graduations, and cultural gatherings. Children will light up to see their pastor at school, and they'll go home saying, "Rev. came to my school today!" That kind of care makes an impact across generations.

- **Serve as a Civic Voice of Godly Wisdom**

Get involved in civic affairs. Join town meetings, advocate on issues impacting your community, and organize forums for awareness and training. Your voice should ring out especially when justice, fairness, and the well-being of the community are at risk. Speak up when others cannot. Stand strong when others are silent.

- **Build Bridges Through Relationships**

Visit homes when invited. Get to know community members personally. When you connect with people's hearts, you win their trust. Over time, the community will say, "*That's my pastor, too,*" even if they're not a member of your church. And when conflict or gossip arises, they'll be the first to defend your integrity.

- **Teach, Don't Just Talk**

Offer biblical instruction on social issues from the pulpit, but also create community-based training sessions that address real-life concerns: education, health, justice, housing, and youth development. Let people know God cares about every part of their lives, and so do you.

HOW and WHEN Should the Minister's Voice Be Heard in the Community?

WHEN:
- When injustice is present
- When families are hurting
- When children are suffering
- When systems are failing
- When the neighborhood is changing for the worse
- When people are afraid to speak up

HOW:
- Through preaching that speaks to the times
- Through personal visits and check-ins
- Through community-led forums and partnerships
- Through public presence at meetings and events
- Through relationships rooted in compassion and truth
- Through the internet that every adult and child sees

The story of Humpty Dumpty is often told to children as a rhyme, but it carries a sobering truth for us today:

"All the king's horses and all the king's men couldn't put Humpty Dumpty back together again."

This line echoes the tragic inability of government and political systems to truly heal or restore our broken communities. Policies, programs, and platforms may attempt to fix the issues, but they can never reach the soul of a person or the heart of a neighborhood.

Yet while the government struggles to make lasting change, the family of God has become unwilling, or unaware, of the divine power we've been given to transform lives and situations through the authority of Jesus Christ.

Jesus gave us clear authority, and yet when I look around, I am troubled. We have plenty of churches on every corner in some cities, and yet the enemy still abuses our communities. How can this be?

It's because the Church must be built on more than tradition or personality. Jesus said, "Upon this rock I will build my church, and the gates of hell shall not prevail against it" (Matthew 16:18). That *"rock"* is not Peter the man, but a foundational truth, Christ Himself.

The "gates of hell" are the social ills that plague our communities:

- Poverty
- Racism
- Addiction
- Violence
- Broken families

To confront these gates, we need a recognized spiritual authority. Jesus said in verse 19:

"And I will give you the keys of the kingdom of heaven: whatever you bind on earth will be bound in heaven, and whatever you loose on earth will be loosed in heaven."

"Binding and loosing" were rabbinical terms meaning to forbid or permit, but only those in authority could do so.

In Acts 19, the seven sons of Sceva *tried* to exercise authority they had not been given. The evil spirit exposed their lack of power and left them wounded and humiliated. This story reminds us that spiritual authority must be recognized by both heaven and hell.

The church cannot simply speak about authority, we must walk in it. We must be a church that is both anointed and authentic.

Despite society's growing skepticism, the church is still critically necessary. Sadly, many unchurched people, 81% by some studies, believe the church is insensitive to their real needs. And to be honest, we must take some responsibility for that perception.

How are we presenting ourselves? What are we known for?

The church is *not* a museum for the perfect. It is a hospital for the broken. We are all patients seeking the Great Physician's healing hand. And we have a mission:

1. **To Bring Order to Our Lives**
We are out of order without God.
- Worship Order - There is a difference between noise and true worship that honors God.
- Home Order - Many homes today are spiritually and emotionally broken. Some should hang a sign saying, "Out of Order."
- Personal Order - We need lives marked by holiness, discipline, and obedience.

2. **To Be the Voice of Righteousness**
We've been given the keys to the Kingdom. That means we have access, authority, and responsibility. The church must be:
- Salt and Light
- Vocal in righteousness
- Concerned not just with internal gatherings but with external transformation

We are not just called to have church... **we are called to be the Church.**

3. **To Preach the Gospel of Jesus Christ**
More than ever, we need the power of the Gospel:
- Our children are being consumed by the scourge of drugs
- Our families are being devastated by divorce
- Our communities are collapsing under moral decay
- Our schools are plagued by violence and fear
- Same sex marriages
- Children confused about who they are

Only Jesus can restore what is broken. And only the church can proclaim that message in the streets, schools, homes, and hearts.

In these troubled times, the community is looking not for a perfect church, but for a present and powerful one. The minister must rise as a voice for those who have no voice. The church must reclaim its purpose. And we must all walk in our God-given authority, not with arrogance, but with assurance.

The gates of hell may be loud, but they will not prevail against a church that stands on the Rock.

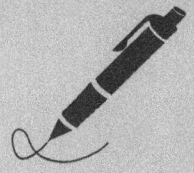

Lord, help us be a Church that is bold, compassionate, and committed. Teach us to walk in authority, speak truth in love, and be a light in the darkest places.

Amen.

66

Isaiah 11:6

The wolf also shall dwell with the lamb, and the leopard shall lie down with the kid; and the calf and the young lion and the fatling together; and a little child shall lead them.

chapter eight

Chapter Eight - A MESSAGE TO YOUNG CLERGY

"Study to shew thyself approved unto God, a workman that needeth not to be ashamed, rightly dividing the word of truth. But shun profane and vain babblings: for they will increase unto more ungodliness." -2 Timothy 2:15–16 (KJV)

To every young clergy member called into pastoral leadership: your voice matters. Not just for the future church, but for the church now. ***Your presence, your passion, and your spiritual insight are needed in the pulpit, in planning rooms, and among the people.***

When you say "*yes*" to this sacred call, prepare to walk a road that isn't always easy. You will be misunderstood, criticized, opposed, accused, and sometimes even rejected. That comes with the assignment. But you're not in this alone. Find two or three seasoned clergy who have been in ministry for some time. Sit with them. Ask questions. Share your heart. Learn from both their victories and their scars.

Also, seek out a trustworthy lay member, someone who loves God, loves the church, and desires to see the congregation grow in service and faith. Their wisdom and honesty will ground you when leadership feels lonely.

The Four Marks of a Faithful Minister

- **Reverence**

When we step into the sanctuary, we stand on holy ground. As clergy, we must never lose the awe of leading God's people in worship. Be real. Be honest with yourself and with the congregation, you don't have all the answers, and that's okay. There are faithful, gifted members sitting in the pews, ready to help. You don't need to do it all.

In this contemporary age, we sometimes lose our sense of sacredness. But the sanctuary is not just another room, it's where heaven meets earth. Worship should be God-centered, Spirit-led, and filled with awe. Take time to plan worship thoughtfully. Let it be relevant, yes, but also reverent. Accessible, yes, but also holy. Let it rise upward to honor the One who is holy and worthy of our best praise. And stay in prayer, always seeking divine wisdom and the leading of the Holy Spirit.

- **Instruction**

As a pastor, your primary calling is to point people to the truth. That means preaching and teaching the Word of God with conviction, clarity, and consistency. Study the scriptures, pray earnestly, and strive to be a fountain of living water, not a stagnant pool.

Good pastors are readers, listeners, and learners. Stay informed. Read the newspaper. Attend city and school board meetings. Be present at civic events. Observe what's happening in the streets and on social media, and apply it to the Gospel of Jesus Christ. People want to know that their pastor is in touch with God, and in touch with the times.

- **Conduct**

Your life will speak louder than your sermons. Live holy. Live honestly. Let your walk match your talk. People are watching, not because they expect perfection, but because they hope for authenticity.

Our lifestyle should turn people toward God. Remind them, lovingly and often, that how we live matters. As pastors, we are wounded healers. We minister out of our own pain, not from a pedestal. Before you can wipe someone else's tears, you must first learn to weep.

Let your conduct *preach* the Gospel even when you're silent.

- **Protection**

The ministry is a battlefield. And prayer is your armor. Without a strong prayer life and firm biblical convictions, a pastor can drift into simply being a religious social worker. But we are more than that, we are guardians of God's Word.

Cling to the scriptures. Walk closely with God. Teach and preach from the foundation of His truth. Prayer is what will protect you from temptation and spiritual burnout.

The old church used to sing:
"*Somebody prayed for me, had me on their mind, took the time and prayed for me...*"
Whether it was your mother, a church mother, or an "elder" deacon, they prayed. And now, it's your turn to pray. Pray always. Stay rooted in the Word. Tell the people not just what feels good, but what God has commanded. Live it. Speak it. Model it.

When God calls you into pastoral ministry, He does not promise comfort, but He does promise His presence.

As a young clergy member, it's easy to feel the weight of expectations, both spoken and unspoken. The journey is filled with moments of misunderstanding, criticism, and even loneliness. But take heart: you are not alone. Others have walked this road and are willing to walk with you. Seek them out. Listen. Learn. Grow.

This calling demands more than a title. It calls for reverence in worship, truth in teaching, holiness in conduct, and strength through prayer. Ministry is not performance—it is sacred service.

Even when the path feels uphill, remain faithful. Let your leadership be rooted in prayer, your words seasoned with grace, and your life a reflection of Christ. Your voice matters now—not just for the future church, but for the church today.

Prayer:
Lord, thank You for calling me to serve Your people. Give me the courage to lead with humility, the wisdom to speak truth, and the strength to walk in holiness. Help me seek counsel, stay grounded in Your Word, and remain faithful in prayer. Use me, Lord, to be a light in this generation. In Jesus' name, amen.

chapter nine

Chapter Nine - THE EVALUATION

Yes, the pastor should be evaluated. Not to tear them down, but to build them up. Evaluation, when done prayerfully and respectfully, *is not* criticism. It is an act of love, stewardship, and care for both the leader and the flock.

The pastor is not above accountability. In fact, they should model it.

We often hold church staff, volunteers, ministries, and even Sunday School teachers to some form of evaluation, yet we sometimes avoid evaluating the shepherd. But how can the church grow if its leader is unaware of blind spots, burdens, or unmet needs in the congregation?

An effective evaluation is not about personality, it's about purpose. It should focus on spiritual health, leadership effectiveness, communication clarity, vision alignment, and the condition of the flock. The goal is not perfection, but progress.

Here's what a healthy evaluation can offer:

1. Spiritual Growth and Renewal
An honest check-in helps the pastor reflect on their own walk with God. It's easy to pour into others and never pause to be poured into. Evaluation reminds the pastor that their *personal* relationship with Christ must remain the well they draw from, not the applause of people or the weight of duty.

2. Understanding the Needs of the Congregation
People change. Communities change. A once-thriving program may now need a fresh vision. An effective pastor listens, learns, and leads with understanding.

3. Measuring the Mission: Are We Fulfilling the Vision?

Every church should have a spiritual vision and measurable goals. Are we making disciples? Are souls being saved? Are we serving our community? The evaluation asks: Are we just doing church, or are we being the Church? The pastor plays a central role in this. Regular reflection helps ensure we're not busy but fruitful.

4. Encouraging Growth | Not Just Correction

A healthy evaluation doesn't just point out areas for improvement. It also celebrates victories. It lifts the pastor's arms like Aaron and Hur did for Moses. It reminds the pastor, You are seen. You are appreciated. Keep going.

5. Strengthening the Bond Between Shepherd and Sheep

Evaluation is not a tool for control, it's a tool for connection. When done in love, it draws the pastor and people closer. It creates safe spaces for honest conversations, healthy adjustments, and shared vision.

A pastor who welcomes feedback is a pastor who desires to grow. A church that offers it in love is a church that values healthy leadership.

The goal is not perfection, but alignment with God's will, unity in the body, and fruit that remains.

Let us evaluate with grace, receive with humility, and grow together in the love of Christ.

chapter ten

Chapter Ten - REMEMBER WHERE YOU CAME FROM

"Only be careful, and watch yourselves closely so that you do not forget the things your eyes have seen or let them fade from your heart as long as you live. Teach them to your children and to their children after them." Deuteronomy 4:1-9 (NIV)

As we recently celebrated the birthday of Rev. Dr. Martin Luther King, Jr., and prepared to observe Black History Month, we are reminded of the rich legacy we carry. From Genesis to Revelation, our ancestors are *present* in the pages of Scripture, a testimony that we have always been a part of God's divine story. But if we forget our history, we risk repeating it. And worse, without a personal relationship with God through Jesus Christ, we are bound to wander aimlessly, lost and disconnected from our purpose.

The Apostle Paul, in Philippians 3:3–9, spoke boldly of his heritage. Yet, he considered all of it a loss compared to the surpassing worth of knowing Christ. Likewise, while we must embrace and celebrate our heritage, it should never become a substitute for knowing and living for Jesus.

Dr. King spoke of a Promised Land. And while we've seen some of the doors open to that vision, many of us are still wandering. Why? Not for lack of opportunity, but for lack of direction... spiritual direction. We've *traded* the discipline of our ancestors for destructive cycles of violence, disrespect, drug abuse, and generational trauma. *Too many of our young men are behind bars instead of in classrooms.* Too many of our young women are preparing for motherhood before they've even had a chance to grow themselves. But God has a **better** plan.

We are paying a spiritual and social price for forgetting that every Black boy and girl, and every child, regardless of race, is made in God's image and destined for a purpose. That purpose begins with learning to love God, love others, and respect oneself.

Self-respect empowers us to reject destructive behavior. Disobedience kept many of God's people from entering the *Promised Land*, not because God wasn't willing, but because they weren't ready. The same is true today.

We come from a people who have done mighty things. We've built, we've endured, we've overcome. But somewhere along the way, we've stopped reminding our children of that truth. I remember my Mama and Granddaddy saying, "Remember where you come from." That wasn't just about our home address, it was about honoring the family name, walking with integrity, and carrying ourselves with pride.

Today, I ask you: ***How are you protecting your family's name? Are you walking in a way that brings honor or shame?*** Because it's not just about "*me*," it's about legacy.

Parents, we are the first teachers. It's our job, along with the church, school, community, and government, to provide our children with guidance rooted in God's Word. College isn't for everyone, but that's not an excuse for laziness. We must encourage our youth to pursue technical training, trades, and professions: health care, carpentry, mechanics, law enforcement, HVAC, culinary arts, teaching, law, medicine, entrepreneurship. These are *not* just jobs. They are lifelong, honorable careers.

Once upon a time, we were willing to die for freedom. Now we die for turf. We've turned on one another and stayed silent in the face of wrongdoing. It's time to raise our voices, not in anger, but in truth and love.

Black History doesn't start with slavery. Our story began long before the first slave ships docked. We are descendants of Ham: builders of nations, architects of civilization. We were kings, queens, scientists, and scribes. Our history is filled with excellence, and our faith has always been central.

God constantly reminded Israel to remember: *"When you were slaves, I set you free... I did miracles on your behalf. I brought you out not as slaves, but as a victorious people."* When we remember what God has done, we live with gratitude and purpose.

Short memories produce ungrateful people. Let's not be ungrateful. We didn't get here by ourselves. Our ancestors prayed, fought, sacrificed, and endured so we could stand tall today.

2 Peter 2:15 says, *"And I will make every effort to see that after my departure you will always be able to remember these things."*

So, I close this book with one charge: Remember where you came from.

Not just your hometown, not just your last name, but your spiritual and historical identity. When we remember who we are, we can walk boldly into who we're meant to become.

66

Proverbs 3:1-8

1 My son, forget not my law; but let thine heart keep my commandments:

2 For length of days, and long life, and peace, shall they add to thee.

3 Let not mercy and truth forsake thee: bind them about thy neck; write them upon the table of thine heart:

4 So shalt thou find favour and good understanding in the sight of God and man.

5 Trust in the Lord with all thine heart; and lean not unto thine own understanding.

6 In all thy ways acknowledge him, and he shall direct thy paths.

7 Be not wise in thine own eyes: fear the Lord, and depart from evil.

8 It shall be health to thy navel, and marrow to thy bones.

appendix

Woodland High School Baccalaureate Sermon

First, I would like to thank God. I also want to express my appreciation to the St. George Ministerial Alliance, our school board trustees, the Superintendent of Education, and the Woodland High School Administration for trusting me to bring words of encouragement to the future leaders of this community, our state, this country, and the world. We are all counting on you to make it a better place for God's people.

I remember sitting right where you are now, 53 years ago. I don't remember what the preacher said that day, but I do remember the excitement, the sense of something greater ahead, and the blessing over my life as I approached graduation.

Back then, my thoughts were probably like yours today: "*I'm going to do what I want to do. No more Mama or Granddaddy telling me when to go to bed, what time to wake up, or to eat my breakfast. No more, 'We're going to church,' or, 'Do your homework, get good grades, A's and B's, listen to your teacher because they have what you need. God didn't make any dumb children.*" You remember those sayings. "*Be on time. You're not wearing that. Don't make me ashamed.*" You get it. You've heard it. You've lived it.

When I told my wife and granddaughter, Le'Neria, a freshman at South Carolina State University, that I'd been asked to speak at Woodland's Baccalaureate, my granddaughter asked me, "*What are you going to talk about?*"
I said, "*I don't know yet. I haven't consulted with God.*"

She thought for a moment, then said, "You need to be real. Simple. And short. Just three words so they'll remember it the rest of their lives."

I asked her, "What's that?"

And she said, "Count on me."

That stuck with me. And I want it to stick with you, too.

That's what I told her growing up: *"I'm counting on you to do the Godly thing. The right thing. Be somebody. Don't be the problem, be the problem-solver."*

Isaiah 11:6 says, "And a little child shall lead them."

And Luke 2:52 tells us that Jesus, even as a young boy, "increased in wisdom and stature, and in favor with God and man."

What does that mean for you?

It means your home training matters. What you've been taught at home and in school, good manners, respect, showing up prepared, those things will open doors. People are drawn to those with integrity. Because of your mannerism and appearance, because of your attitude and presence, people will be more inclined to help you, teach you, and support you.

You've heard it said: Your first impression is your lasting impression. The way you look. The way you talk. The way you carry yourself. That's real life.

Yes, it's important to have book knowledge. But it's just as important to have common sense to know how and when to use that knowledge. Make good choices. Remember where you come from. Know the right people to talk to. Respect others. Be in the right places. Show up on time. Help someone else when you can. Don't hurt others.

And most of all, love God, stay connected to the church, feed on His Word, and always pray.

Some of you will enter parenthood early. Some of you will attend 4-year universities. Others will choose 2-year technical colleges, the workforce, the military, or maybe start businesses of their own. Whatever *your path*, do your best. Be your best. We're counting on you to be good at what you do, and even better at who you are.

Say it with me: "*Yes, you can count on me!*"
Because you are the next:
- Parents
- Schoolteachers
- Cooks and dietitians
- Doctors
- Truck drivers
- Principals
- Guidance counselors
- Band directors
- Bankers

And the list goes on.

So I close with this:
We're counting on you.
The world is waiting on you.
And God is calling you.
Count on me.

PASTOR'S DEDICATION

I like to thank the Bishops: Edward Lewis Tullis, Roy Clyde Clark, Joseph Benjamin Bethea, Robert Hitchcock Spain, James Lawrence McCleskey, Mary Virginia Taylor and L. Jonathan Holston for allowing me to serve God's people as a pastor/preacher for 45 years under their administration.

To MY wife, Dearie, thank you for reminding me not to fuss at the people, but **preach** the gospel and sit down because they love you.

My two children, Lenny and Leah, and granddaughter, Le'Neria, who would say every Sunday, "What you are going to preach about daddy", "Keep it simple," and "Talk our language, too." Thank you knuckle heads!

Thank you to my mama, Adelle! Thank you to my best friend and my second mama, Mrs. Eartha Lee Jenning, that would call mama and tell her when I was in the wrong places.

Thanks to my sisters and brothers for encouraging me in their own way. One brother would say, "You're too scared to be a preacher." Three sisters and my other brother would just smile, and the other sister would say, "You better do the right thing."

Too many others to name that prayed for me on my pastoral journey. May God blessings be upon all of you. Amen.

A Leadership Guide to Accountability

Rev. Leonard Huggins, Jr.